Recipes for Readers

Developing Comprehension and Meaning

Grades 3-6

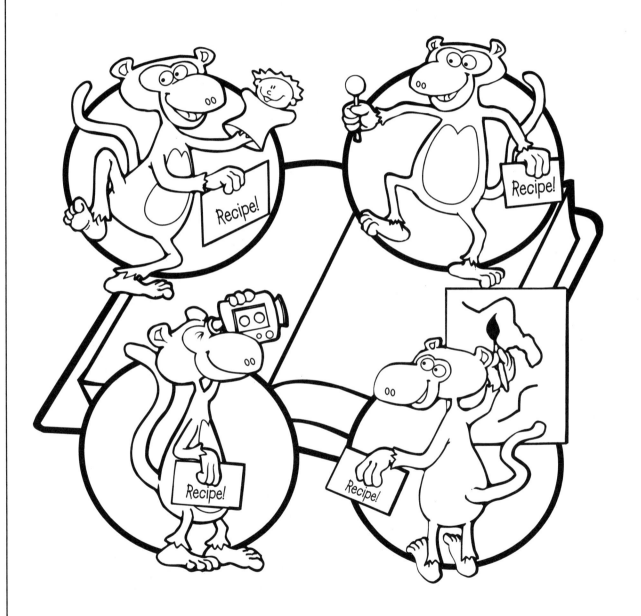

Written by Beth Berridge

Published by World Teachers Press®

Published with the permission of R.I.C. Publications Pty. Ltd.

First published by R.I.C. Publications Pty. Ltd., Perth, Western Australia.

Printed in the United States of America.

Order Number 2-5136
ISBN 1-58324-060-8

A B C D E F 03 02 01 00

Educational Resources
395 Main Street
Rowley, MA 01969
www.worldteacherspress.com

Foreword

Recipes for Readers - Developing Comprehension and Meaning has been developed to help you provide your students with an individualized reading program. The activities allow students to work independently to improve their reading skills, while freeing you to work with those students who need more direct instruction.

The activities in *Recipes for Readers* are based on Bloom's Taxonomy. A group of educational psychologists, headed by Benjamin Bloom, developed the taxonomy in 1956 as a classification of levels of intellectual behavior important in learning. The three domains are cognitive, psychomotor and affective. In the cognitive domain, Bloom identifies the six levels that are used as the basis of this book:

Knowledge and Comprehension
Application
Analysis
Synthesis
Evaluation

The activities move from the simple recall or recognition of facts, at the lowest level, through increasingly more complex and abstract mental levels to the highest order, Evaluation.

Menu

How to Use the Recipes

1. To prepare the Recipes, or activities, for student use, photocopy each page.

2. Create a "Book Board" in the classroom where students may display the posters, written work or artwork of the completed activities.

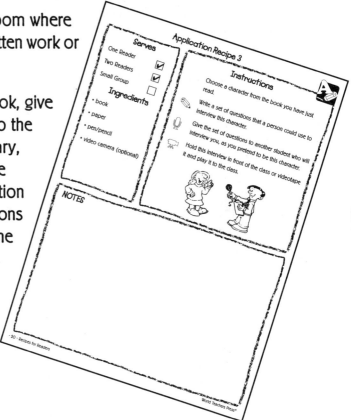

3. After a student finishes reading a book, give the student the Recipe appropriate to the reading level of that book. If necessary, discuss the aim of the Recipe with the student. You can use the "Notes" section of each page to give additional directions to the student or the student may use the section to take notes while working through the activity.

4. The Recipe Record Sheet (page 5) may be maintained to monitor the range and level of the Recipes each student completes.

World Teachers Press®

Recipe Record Sheet

Names	Knowledge and Comprehension												Application										Analysis										Synthesis										Evaluation									
	1	2	3	4	5	6	7	8	9	10	11	12	1	2	3	4	5	6	7	8	9	10	1	2	3	4	5	6	7	8	9	10	1	2	3	4	5	6	7	8	9	10	1	2	3	4	5	6	7	8	9	10

Knowledge and Comprehension Recipe 1

Serves

One Reader ✔

Two Readers ✔

Small Group ☐

Ingredients

• book

• paper

• pen/pencil

• poster paper

• colored pens/pencils

Instructions

Count how many characters there are in the book.

 Write a list of all the characters.

 Ask another student who has read the book to also count the characters and check to see if your results are the same.

Now choose one of these characters and design a character poster to suit.

 At the bottom of your poster write: **Read all about this character in _____ (title) by _____ (author).**

NOTES

World Teachers Press®

K&C

Serves

One Reader ☑

Two Readers ☐

Small Group ☐

Ingredients

• book

• paper

• pen/pencil

• colored pens/pencils

Instructions

Choose a character in the book who has a lot to say.

Decide what the most important thing this character said was and quote it.

Draw a cartoon balloon around this quote then draw the character with the matching expression on his or her face.

On the bottom of your picture write: **Read why this character said this in _____ (title) by _____ (author).**

blah...blah...blah...

NOTES

Knowledge and Comprehension Recipe 3

Serves

One Reader ✔

Two Readers ☐

Small Group ☐

Ingredients

• book

• paper

• colored pens/pencils

• tape

• tape recorder

• transparent plastic bag

Instructions

 Recall the events in the book.

List these in order.

Think about which of these events you could draw.

 Now design a story map for the book.

On tape, record your retelling of the story.

End this with the words: **If you want to know more, read _____ (title) by _____ (author).**

Put this tape and story map into a plastic bag for others to borrow from the class library.

NOTES

World Teachers Press®

Knowledge and Comprehension Recipe 4

Serves

One Reader ☐

Two Readers ☑

Small Group ☐

Ingredients

• book

• paper

• pen/pencil

Instructions

Discuss with another student, who has read the book, which character you think is the most important.

Write down your reasons for making this selection.

Identify the traits of this character then write a character sketch including facts such as who the character is, where he or she lives and what he or she likes to do.

At the bottom of the page write: **Meet this character in _____ (title) by _____ (author).**

NOTES

Knowledge and Comprehension Recipe 5

Serves

One Reader	☑
Two Readers	☐
Small Group	☐

Ingredients

- book

- poster paper and colored pens/pencils

or

- writing paper, pen/pencil and envelope

Instructions

Write what you thought of the book you have just read.

If you like the book, write an advertisement to put on the book board so others will want to read it.

If you did not like the book, write to the author, explaining why and give suggestions on how it could be improved. Check your letter with the teacher before mailing to the publisher, and look forward to the reply.

NOTES

World Teachers Press®

Knowledge and Comprehension Recipe 6

Serves

One Reader ☑

Two Readers ☐

Small Group ☐

Ingredients

- book
- paper
- pen/pencil
- book size art paper
- colored pens/pencils

Instructions

 Note the main points of the book. You may need to refer to the book.

Use these to write a summary of the story that will encourage others to read it.

Design a dust jacket for this book and include your summary.

Put the new jacket on the book and display to encourage others to read the book.

HINT:
Look at the jacket of a hard-covered book to give you an idea of how to lay it out with pictures and text.

NOTES

Knowledge and Comprehension Recipe 7

Serves

One Reader ✔

Two Readers ☐

Small Group ☐

Ingredients

• book

• paper

• poster paper

• colored pens/pencils

• ruler

• example of a plan of a stage set

Instructions

Describe in your own words the setting where most of the action took place in this book.

📖 Pretend you are designing a set for a play based on this book.

✏ On the poster paper, draw a diagram, labeling it in such a way that the stagehands could set the stage to look like the setting.

HINT:
You may need to look at some plays in the library to get an idea of how this diagram could be drawn.

NOTES

World Teachers Press®

Knowledge and Comprehension Recipe 8

K&C

Serves

One Reader ✔

Two Readers ☐

Small Group ☐

Ingredients

- book
- tape and tape recorder

  or

- 8 ½" x 11" paper folded to make a book
- poster paper
- colored pens/pencils

Instructions

Tell part or all of the story again but change the characters around so the villain is now the hero and the hero, the villain.

 You may like to tell your story on tape for listening, or write it, presenting it like a book for others to borrow and read.

 Design an advertisement for your story to encourage others to read or listen to it.

I'm a good guy now, honest!

NOTES

Knowledge and Comprehension Recipe 9

Serves

One Reader ✔

Two Readers ☐

Small Group ☐

Ingredients

• book

• paper

• long piece of paper

• cards

• pens/pencils

Instructions

📖 Outline the main events in the book.

Make a timeline that indicates the sequence of these events on the long piece of paper.

✏️ Write these events on cards and design a game that uses your timeline.

NOTES

World Teachers Press®

Knowledge and Comprehension Recipe 10

Serves

One Reader ✔

Two Readers ☐

Small Group ☐

Ingredients

- book

- examples of similar articles from magazines

- colored pens/pencils

- paper

- personal photos

Instructions

Pretend you are the author of the book.

 Write an article for a magazine, outlining the story and explaining why you wrote it.

 Present this article like you would see in a magazine, including drawings or photographs with captions.

Put your article on the class book board under an eye-catching headline.

HINT:
Sometimes authors use events that really happened in their lives.

NOTES

Knowledge and Comprehension Recipe 11

Serves

One Reader ✔

Two Readers ☐

Small Group ☐

Ingredients

- book
- example of report card
- pen/pencil
- paper
- markers

Instructions

Name all the characters in the book.

Briefly describe one of the characters.

Think about the character's actions and reactions.

Decide which of this information would be useful to write a report card for this character.

Design a report card like the one used by your school.

Fill in the report card, making up the school and teacher.

Display the report card on the class book board under an eye-catching heading, for example, **Brilliant New Pupil.**

NOTES

World Teachers Press®

K&C

Serves

One Reader ☑

Two Readers ☐

Small Group ☐

Ingredients

- book
- paper
- graph paper
- colored pens/pencils

Instructions

Give a brief outline of the story, listing the main events in order.

Work out a five-point rating scale, such as 1 - not exciting (background material), and 5 - very exciting.

Now rate the excitement of each event and plot it on a graph. You can use a pie graph, a bar graph, line graph or a column graph.

Put your graph on the book board under the heading: **Have the excitement of your lifetime with** _____ **(title) written by** _____ **(author).**

NOTES

Application Recipe 1

Serves

One Reader ✔

Two Readers ☐

Small Group ☐

Ingredients

• book

• paper

• art paper

• colored pens/pencils

Instructions

Use the ending of this book to make up another story.

 When you have completed your first draft, decide which portions of the story you would like to illustrate.

Now divide your text to match these illustrations and present it as a small picture book.

 Display your book on a stand with an eye-catching advertisement to attract students to read your book. (Authors often hold a party to launch their books.)

HINT:
The number of pages in all picture books is divisible by 8.

NOTES

World Teachers Press®

Application Recipe 2

Serves

One Reader ✔

Two Readers ☐

Small Group ☐

Ingredients

• book

• paper

• pen/pencil

Instructions

 The author of the book you have just read used a beginning to attract your attention to make you want to read on. Decide how the author did this and apply this knowledge by following the author's recipe to write a beginning to a story.

Put your beginning on the book board under the heading: **Story Starters.**

NOTES

Application Recipe 3

Serves

One Reader   ☑

Two Readers   ☑

Small Group   ☐

Ingredients

• book

• paper

• pen/pencil

• video camera (optional)

Instructions

Choose a character from the book you have just read.

 Write a set of questions that a person could use to interview this character.

 Give the set of questions to another student who will interview you, as you pretend to be this character.

 Hold this interview in front of the class or videotape it and play it to the class.

NOTES

Serves

One Reader ☑

Two Readers ☐

Small Group ☑

Ingredients

- book

- paper

  or

- materials to make

  puppets and backdrop

Instructions

 Choose an interesting part of the story that has a lot of speech in it. Use this speech to dramatize this scene from your book, using a storyteller if required.

 Choose members of your class to be the actors. Practice the play and present it to the class.

- OR -

Make a set of puppets and a backdrop to go with your script. Perform the play for the class, then put your puppets and script in a box labeled with the title of your play and give the kit to the library.

NOTES

Application Recipe 5

Serves

One Reader ☑

Two Readers ☐

Small Group ☑

Ingredients

• book

• poster paper

• colored pens/pencils

• box for storage

Instructions

List the main events in the book. (A story map could help you.)

Think about board or card games you have enjoyed playing. What made them fun? How were they played?

Choose a game that would suit the story. Using the main events, construct a board or card game. Try it out on a small group of students who have read the book.

HINT:
Look at a board game to get ideas on design and rules.

Improve it if necessary and pack it in a suitable box so others can borrow it. Place it in a lending spot.

NOTES

World Teachers Press®

Application Recipe 6

Serves

One Reader ☑

Two Readers ☐

Small Group ☑

Ingredients

- book
- cards
- paper
- pen/pencil
- box

Instructions

 Based on the book you have just read, develop a set of questions on cards.

Place these in a box with a set of rules for playing.

Design an eye-catching cover for the box with suggested suitable ages for players.

 Test the game with a group of students that have also read this book.

Make changes if required to improve the game.

Present the game to the library to be borrowed with the book.

HINT:
Look at other games for ideas.

NOTES

Application Recipe 7

Serves

One Reader ☑

Two Readers ☐

Small Group ☐

Ingredients

• book

• poster paper

• lined exercise book for diary

• poster paper

• colored pens/pencils

Instructions

✎ Choose a character in the book and list, in time sequence, all the events that happened to him/her.

Imagine you are this character.

✎ Write your personal diary using these events as entries. Title it: **The Private Diary of _____ .**

Devise a puzzle question that students must answer to allow them to read your diary. This could be a password, a riddle, a cryptogram, an acrostic, an anagram, a rebus or a word/message hidden in a picture.

HINT:
Use a book for your diary then cover it in cloth with a little padding on the front and back. Design a fancy label to make your book look special.

Make a poster saying: **Think you're smart? Figure this out to be able to read "The Private Diary of ...."**

NOTES

World Teachers Press®

Application Recipe 8

Serves

One Reader ☑

Two Readers ☐

Small Group ☐

Ingredients

- book
- colored pens/pencils
- paper
- materials to make a diorama
- tape
- tape recorder

Instructions

Recall your favorite setting in the book.

List all the important features of this setting then draw a sketch labeling these features, for example, *an icy cold breeze chilled his neck (an arrow points to the character's neck).*

Use this sketch to make a diorama of this setting.

On a tape, using background music and sound effects, read the part of the text that describes the setting. Set up the tape recorder alongside your diorama so people can view and listen.

NOTES

Application Recipe 9

Serves

One Reader ✔

Two Readers ☐

Small Group ☐

Ingredients

• book

• paper

• 8 ½" x 11" paper cut in half lengthwise

• pen/pencil

Instructions

Calculate how many different events occurred in the book.

 List them in the order they occurred.

Construct a timeline for these events using several pieces of paper joined end to end.

At each point on the line, provide information about when, where, what and who were involved in each event, as well as an illustration.

Fold your timeline and place it in the inside cover of the book or put it on the book board with the book displayed below and an eye-catching heading saying: **Pass your time with _____ (title).**

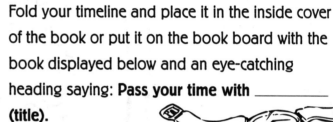

NOTES

World Teachers Press®

Application Recipe 10

Serves

One Reader ✔

Two Readers ☐

Small Group ☐

Ingredients

- book
- example of newspaper article
- paper
- computer/word processor
- photocopier

Instructions

Write a newspaper article on an important incident in the book.

Include a headline to capture attention, date and place. Use a lead sentence to encourage the reader to read on. Follow with details of who, what, why, how and when. Finish off with a compelling conclusion.

Type your story on the computer, presenting it like a real newspaper article. Photocopy your article and distribute for others to read. Don't forget to include information about the title and author of this book in case your newspaper article encourages them to read it.

NOTES

Analysis Recipe 1

Serves

One Reader ☑

Two Readers ☐

Small Group ☐

Ingredients

• book

• paper

• pen/pencil

• art paper

• colored pens/pencils

Instructions

Compare two characters in the book.

In what ways are they the same? In what ways are they different?

 Pretend you are a book critic. Write a paper using this comparison to explain why you prefer one of the characters over the other.

Design an award for this character and present it after you have read your paper to the class.

HINT:
You could use ideas from award presentation ceremonies on TV.

NOTES

Analysis Recipe 2

Serves

One Reader ☑

Two Readers ☐

Small Group ☑

Ingredients

• narrative story

• paper

• pen/pencil

• audio tape and recorder

• box

Instructions

 In a narrative, authors often use contrasts, for example, *stillness and a sudden noise* or *good and evil characters.* Make a list of all the contrasts the author has used in a narrative story you have recently read.

Make an audio tape with sound effects and music accompanying your reading of the list.

Design a presentation cover for a box to hold your tape.

Prepare a short talk to introduce it, then play the tape to the class or a group in the library.

NOTES

Analysis Recipe 3

Serves

One Reader ☑

Two Readers ☐

Small Group ☐

Ingredients

• narrative story

• paper

• pen/pencil

• poster paper

• colored pens/pencils

Instructions

In a narrative, authors use a sequence of ideas to build up excitement and tension. Analyze the narrative to discover the sequence of happenings that built up the tension in the reader.

Present this list of happenings as a recipe for writing an exciting story.

Put an advertisement on the book board for your successful recipe, for example, *Do you want to make a lot of money by being a successful author? Contact _____ for the recipe.*

Have copies of your recipe ready to respond to the requests.

NOTES

World Teachers Press®

Analysis Recipe 4

Serves

One Reader   ☑

Two Readers   ☐

Small Group   ☑

Ingredients

- several books
- paper
- pen/pencil
- cards
- box to store game

Instructions

 List as many characters as you can from books you have read.

Group them according to their characteristics, for example, *bravery* or *beauty.* You will have to work out your own groupings according to the attributes of the characters you have chosen.

 Now write a set of "Who am I?" questions for each character, for example,*"I am a boy. I have an appetite for worms. Who am I?"*

 Design a game using these questions and your character groupings.

 Write instructions for your game, then try it out with other students. Improve it, if necessary, before giving it to the library.

NOTES

Serves

One Reader ✔

Two Readers ☐

Small Group ☐

Ingredients

• book

• paper

• pen/pencil

Instructions

 List all the characters in the book.

Put them in order according to your preference, for example, *the characters you most like to the ones you least like.*

 Survey others who have read the book and ask them to put the characters in order according to their preference.

Now rate the characters according to their popularity, including comments on why this is so. Display your ratings on the book board.

> HINT:
> You could use a star rating system, like they use for TV movies awarding a lemon for the worst.

NOTES

Serves

One Reader ✔

Two Readers ☐

Small Group ☐

Ingredients

• book

• newspaper (entertainment pages)

• poster paper

• colored pens/pencils

Instructions

Examine the book to pick out the main ideas. Decide which of these would attract a reader.

Look in the newspaper to see how films are advertised. Pretend your book has been made into a movie. Design an advertisement for the movie.

Display your advertisement with the book in the library. Judge the success of your advertisement by the number of people who read the book.

HINT:
Ask people to sign an opinion rating list after they have read it. This will keep a tally of the readers.

NOTES

Serves

One Reader ✔

Two Readers ☐

Small Group ☐

Ingredients

• book

• art paper

• writing paper

• pen/pencil

Instructions

Choose two characters from the book. How is each similar to the other?

 Draw a diagram of each, labeling the similarities.

 Pretend you are one of these characters. Write an advertisement to go in the Pen Pal Pages of a newspaper. List your attributes, occupation and interests.

Now pretend you are the other character and write a letter in reply. Display the diagrams, advertisement and reply letter on the book board under the heading: **Perfect Match**.

NOTES

Serves

One Reader ✔

Two Readers ☐

Small Group ✔

Ingredients

• book

• paper

• pen/pencil

• video camera (optional)

Instructions

Think about the story. What's the title? Who are the characters? What is the setting, the action, the outcome? Ask yourself who? what? where? when? questions.

Using this information, write a TV commercial for this book. Choose some friends and act this commercial for the class **OR** you could videotape it to play to the class.

NOTES

Analysis Recipe 9

Serves

One Reader   ☑

Two Readers   ☐

Small Group   ☐

Ingredients

• several books by same author

• paper

• pen/pencil

• computer or typewriter

Instructions

Read several books by the same author.

Under its title, list the main events in each story.

Now compare the events. Are the stories similar? In what ways are they similar?

Using this information, write a story in the style of this author, for example, *the author may always write about some children who have an adventure and help the police.* You will then write a similar story.

Present your story as a serial, typed and displayed on the book board. After each episode write: **Do you want to know what happens to _____ ? Read the next exciting episode of _____ .**

NOTES

World Teachers Press®

Analysis Recipe 10

Serves

One Reader ✔

Two Readers ☐

Small Group ☐

Ingredients

• book

• example of a police report

• pen/pencil

• paper

Instructions

Decide who is the character you dislike most in the book.

Investigate this character noting all the unpleasant things, for example, *description, distinguishing features* or *crimes past and present.*

Using this information, write a police report for this character. Include a photograph or sketch for easy identification.

Display this report with the book.

Invite other readers to write reports on the other characters in the book so there is a whole collection on display.

NOTES

Synthesis Recipe 1

Serves

One Reader ☑

Two Readers ☐

Small Group ☐

Ingredients

• book

• paper

• pen/pencil

• poster paper

• colored pens/pencils

• computer or typewriter

Instructions

How did the book you have just read end? What lead up to this ending? Which characters were involved?

Plan another ending to this book.

Select a paragraph near the end of the story from where your ending will continue.

At the top of your typed and edited ending write: **Alternative ending that continues on from paragraph _____ on page _____** . Place your ending inside the back cover of the book.

Display the book with an advertisement saying: **A story with two endings. If you don't like the first, try the alternative.**

NOTES

World Teachers Press®

Synthesis Recipe 2

Serves

One Reader ✔

Two Readers ☐

Small Group ☐

Ingredients

• book

• writing paper

• pen/pencil

• poster paper

• colored pens/pencils

Instructions

Did you enjoy the book you have just read? Predict how many copies of the book have been sold (record this number). Write to the publisher saying you enjoyed the book and asking how many copies have been sold up-to-date. Compare this number with your prediction.

Design a poster stating: **Did you know that _____ copies of _____ have been sold? Be another reader of this book.**

Display the book below the poster.

NOTES

Synthesis Recipe 3

Serves

One Reader ☑

Two Readers ☐

Small Group ☑

Ingredients

• book

• paper

• pen/pencil

• instruments to use for sound effects

• tape

• tape recorder

Instructions

 Select a part of the book that has several characters having a conversation. Make this into a radio play using a narrator, sound effects, music and different voices for the characters (ask several friends or members of your family to help you).

 You will need to write a script indicating the character's parts and the different sound effects required.

Produce and tape the play, then present it to the class.

NOTES

Synthesis Recipe 4

Serves

One Reader ✔

Two Readers ☐

Small Group ☐

Ingredients

• book

• materials for collage

• glue

• poster paper

Instructions

List all the memorable things about the book you have just read.

Draw sketches of these, then use them to design a collage that represents your memories of the story.

Display this collage in the library with an inspirational title.

NOTES

Synthesis Recipe 5

Serves

One Reader	☑
Two Readers	☐
Small Group	☑

Ingredients

- book
- art paper
- pen/pencil

Instructions

Think about the characters in the book. What problems did they encounter?

 Imagine what they could have done if they had a special device (magical or otherwise).

Invent a device that would assist one of the characters. Name it, then draw a diagram labeling its parts.

List the various ways the device could be used.

Plan how you will market this device. What attributes would attract buyers? Prepare a one-

  minute TV advertisement to sell this invention. You may like to ask some friends to help you.

NOTES

World Teachers Press®

Synthesis Recipe 6

Serves

One Reader ✔

Two Readers ☐

Small Group ☐

Ingredients

- book
- paper
- pen/pencil
- example of a newspaper article showing headlines and captions
- photocopier

Instructions

✎ List the characters in the book and write next to each how they contribute to the plot, for example, *the giant's wife adds to the excitement with warnings to Jack about the giant.*

✎ Combine two of the characters and tell how this would affect the story; for example, *what would happen if two opposing characters united?* Use this idea to write a newspaper article.

Publish it with headlines and captions under a picture to look like a real newspaper.

Photocopy your article for distribution to the class.

NOTES

Synthesis Recipe 7

Serves

One Reader ☑

Two Readers ☐

Small Group ☐

Ingredients

- book
- paper
- music
- tape
- tape recorder
- box for storage
- colored pens/pencils

Instructions

Select a part of the story that appeals to your imagination. Brainstorm feelings you have as you read this section.

 Use these ideas to write a poem. Select appropriate background music.

Read your poem onto a tape using the music as a background. Play your tape to the class, then present it to the library in a box for which you have designed an appropriate cover.

NOTES

Synthesis Recipe 8

Serves

One Reader ✔

Two Readers ☐

Small Group ☐

Ingredients

• book

• paper

• pen/pencil

• photocopier

Instructions

Create a comic strip based on the book you have just read.

Produce it in serial form, putting each episode on the book board under a suitable, eye-catching sign.

HINT:
Cartoonists often save time by photocopying parts of their drawings so they don't have to redraw them each time.

NOTES

Synthesis Recipe 9

Serves

One Reader

Two Readers ☐

Small Group ☐

Ingredients

- book
- paper
- colored pens/pencils
- markers

Instructions

Think of an incident involving the characters in the book. What did they look like? How did they react? Could you change this situation to make it more amusing?

Create a cartoon based on this incident. Use it to make a poster advertising the book. Display this with the book in the library or book corner.

NOTES

World Teachers Press®

Synthesis Recipe 10

Serves

One Reader ☑

Two Readers ☐

Small Group ☐

Ingredients

• book

• materials for making a game or product

• paper

• colored pens/pencils

Instructions

Imagine you are the author of a book, wanting to sell more copies. Develop a new game or product which will promote your book.

After you have made a prototype of your product, plan a marketing strategy. After checking with your teacher, send a copy to the publishers of the book with a letter asking them if they are interested in your product and marketing strategy.

HINT:
Look at how the big film corporations promote their films.

NOTES

Evaluation Recipe 1

Serves

One Reader ✔

Two Readers ☐

Small Group ☐

Ingredients

• book

• writing paper

• pen/pencil

Instructions

What parts of the book did you enjoy?

Do you have you a friend or relative that also likes to read?

Write a letter to this person recommending the book. Include a brief outline of the story and reasons why they should read it.

After showing the letter to your teacher, mail it and look forward to their reply.

NOTES

World Teachers Press®

Evaluation Recipe 2

Serves

One Reader   ☑

Two Readers   ☐

Small Group   ☑

Ingredients

• book

• writing paper

• pen/pencil

Instructions

Find out which students in your school/class have read the book you have just finished. Write to four, inviting them to participate in a panel to discuss the book. Ask each person to decide why they chose it and what they liked or disliked about the book.

With your teacher, arrange a time to hold this panel discussion with the class. Organize the panel so each person has two minutes to outline their ideas about the book, then answer questions from the class.

You be the chairperson for this discussion, introduce the panel members, facilitate the questioning and finally thank the panel, the teacher and the audience for their participation.

NOTES

Evaluation Recipe 3

Serves

One Reader ☑

Two Readers ☐

Small Group ☐

Ingredients

• book

• writing paper

• pen/pencil

Instructions

List the characters in the book.

Choose one character you believe is not important to the story. Pretend you are this character who is under the threat of losing his or her part in the story because the author wants to economize.

Write to the author pointing out all the reasons why you should remain in the story and justify your position as being important.

Display your letter under the headline: **Character under threat of job loss.** Next to it have a copy of a petition, supporting this character's position, for classmates to sign.

NOTES

World Teachers Press®

Evaluation Recipe 4

Serves

One Reader ✔

Two Readers ☐

Small Group ☐

Ingredients

• book

• card for bookmark

• pen/pencil

• paper

• colored pens/pencils

Instructions

Make a collection of books you have read.

 Write a short evaluation for each book pointing out the strong and weak parts. Make a bookmark for each book and write your evaluation on it. Display this collection, with bookmarks attached, near an advertisement encouraging others to read.

 Design a survey form for the readers to evaluate and give their opinions of the books. Decide on some sort of prize to encourage people to read and answer the survey.

NOTES

Evaluation Recipe 5

Serves

One Reader ✔

Two Readers ✔

Small Group ☐

Ingredients

• book

• paper

• pen/pencil

Instructions

 Think about the book and decide why another person should read it. Prepare a debate on: **The reasons you must not miss this book.**

 Find a friend who has not read the book and ask them to prepare the other side of the debate on: **Why I don't want to read that book.**

Arrange a time with your teacher to hold the debate. You will also need someone to judge the debate.

NOTES

World Teachers Press®

Evaluation Recipe 6

Serves

One Reader

Two Readers ✔

Small Group ✔

Ingredients

- book
- paper
- pen/pencil

Instructions

 Select a book that you disliked. Make notes about why you dislike it. Justify your reasons with excerpts from the text.

 Find a person that enjoyed the book. Ask them to make notes on why they thought it was good and to justify their opinion.

 Pretend you are lawyers for the plaintiff and defense. The class is the jury and the teacher, the judge. Hold a court case with the book on trial.

NOTES

Evaluation Recipe 7

Serves

One Reader ✔

Two Readers ✔

Small Group ☐

Ingredients

• book

• paper

• pen/pencil

Instructions

List all the books you have read in the past three months. Next to each title briefly outline what sort of book it is, for example, *information*, *mystery*, *poetry* or *adventure*. Think about these books and decide what type of reader you are.

Set a goal for yourself, for example, *you may decide to read two types of books you haven't read before*. Decide on a reward you will give yourself when you have achieved this goal. Tell someone of your plans and ask them to be your encourager.

Note:
An encourager is someone who says good things about what you are doing. They use words like "Don't worry, you're doing fine!" or "Look you've nearly read the whole book. Well done!"

Go! Go! Go!

NOTES

World Teachers Press®

Evaluation Recipe 8

Serves

One Reader ☑

Two Readers ☐

Small Group ☐

Ingredients

- book
- tape
- tape recorder
- paper
- pen/pencil
- photocopier

Instructions

Authors often express their personal values in a book. Reflecting on a book you have recently read, can you find what the author believes is important? Do you agree with his/her beliefs?

Use this information to compose a song promoting or disagreeing with these beliefs. Tape your song to play to the class. Photocopy the words so your classmates can sing along with the tape.

NOTES

Serves

One Reader   ☑

Two Readers   ☐

Small Group   ☑

Ingredients

• several books

• paper

• pen/pencil

• photocopier (optional)

Instructions

 Form a group and ask each member to bring a book they have recently read. Chair a discussion which starts with each member briefly outlining their book then discussing their feelings about it and any lessons they may have learned.

Conclude the discussion with a short report (given by you) of the feelings and lessons learned by the group.

 Read this report to the whole class **OR** write it as a newspaper report, photocopying it and distributing it to interested students.

NOTES

Evaluation Recipe 10

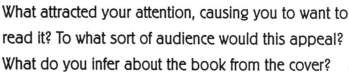

Serves

One Reader ✔

Two Readers ☐

Small Group ☐

Ingredients

• book

• art paper size of a book jacket

• colored pens/pencils

Instructions

 Look at the cover of the book you have just read. What attracted your attention, causing you to want to read it? To what sort of audience would this appeal? What do you infer about the book from the cover?

Design another jacket to cover the book. Decide upon the audience you want to attract and what you want your audience to expect from the book.

 Place this new jacket over the old cover and display your book in an attractive manner. Note how successful your new cover is by the number of people who pick up and look through the book.

HINT:
Look at how book stores display new books in their windows.

NOTES

Coming Down

ff

cli __ __

o __ __

pu __ __

cu __ __

steep

cliff

sh

wi __ __

ru __ __

ca __ __

di __ __

rope

"Hang on. I'm coming!"

This is a steep cli __ __ .

I wi __ __ I was on that

rope, going down that

cli __ __ .

Draw the dog coming down on the rope.

Puzzling

one
①2 3 4

d __ __ __

n __ __ __

__ __ __ s

(eyes)

ere

h __ __ __

th __ __ __

wh __ __ __

w __ __ __

(points)

Here is a pu __ __ le for your eyes.

There is one star hid __ __ __ here.

But wh __ __ __ is it?

Can you find the st __ __ ?

The star has five p __ __ __ __ __ .

It is made up of lots of small sh __ __ __ __ .

It is very, very dif __ __ __ __ __ __ to see.

(shapes)

(puzzle)

Here is a help for your eyes.

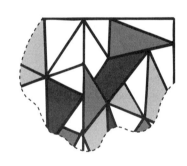

The star is in here.

(hidden)

Here is the answer.

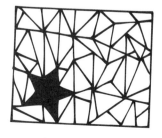

It is upside down.

diff i cult
difficult

diff er ent
different

Think!

If all the shapes had been the same color, the puzzle would be:

(a)   easier.

(b)   more difficult.

(c)   just the same.

Flying

igh

high

l __ __ __ t

br __ __ __ t

fl __ __ __ t

n __ __ __ t

rock ets
rockets

some
come

colors

ou
around
cloud

y

fly

sk __

b __

m __

wh __

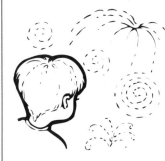

We all like to see fi __ __ works.

Some f __ __ __ w __ __ __ __ shoot sparks

of bright col __ __ s.

Some spin around and ar __ __ __ __ .

fire works
fireworks

But best of all are the

ro __ __ __ __ __ .

Bang! Off they go.

They fly up hi __ __ into the sky.

Ba __ __ ! Look at the bri __ __ __

colors in the dark n __ __ __ t.

Roc __ __ __ __ __ are the best.

ar
star
sparks
park
dark

Colors!

R __ __ sparks

Gr __ __ n li __ __ ts

Ye __ __ ow stars

Bl __ __ flashes

P __ __ k clouds

Wh __ te sm __ ke

Exploring

Sample Page from World Teachers Press' *Literacy Lifters* Book 3

old
older

g_____en

b_____ly

h_____ing

f_____ed

c_____er

symbols   wreck   explore   island

Here's an island for you to exp_____ . There are

rivers and some high hills on your is_____ . There

are lots of trees and a soggy swamp where herons (birds

with long l_____) live. Swarms of bees buzz in the

w_____ sunshine and frogs croak at night.

Hundreds of seabirds nest on ledges in the cliffs. Rabbits

seem to be everywhere. There is a large, dark cave on your

i_____ where people used to live. You can still see the black

stones around their old f_____ . What else do you find in the ca____ ?

wa
was

_____sps

_____rm

_____shes

_____nder

_____lking

_____ter

s_____mp

s_____rm

north
south
east
west

West
Bay

Island

River

Bay

Scale
5km

Legend

▲ trees

An old shipw_____ can be seen at low tide.

What do you find in the wreck? _____

What food will you eat? _____

Exploring

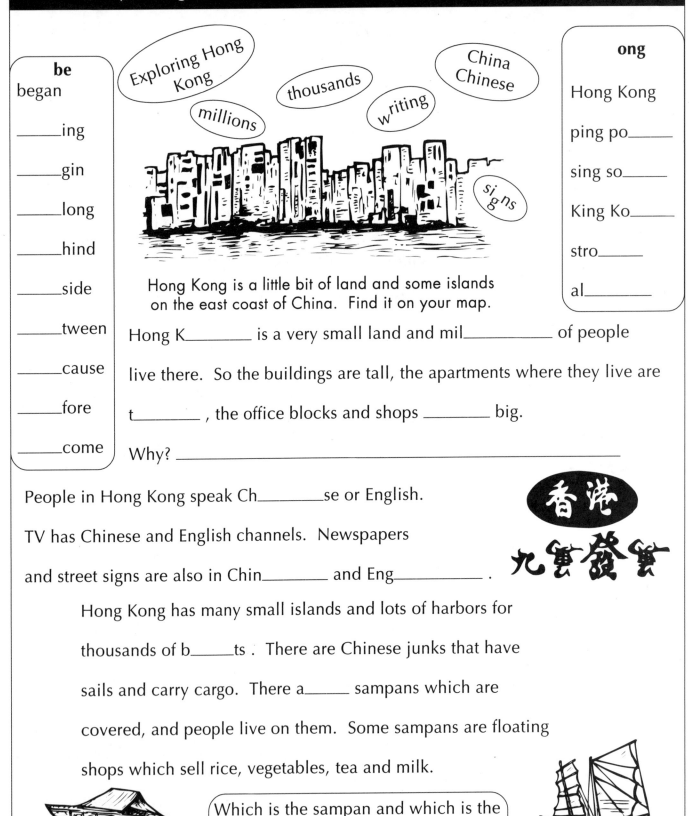

be
began
_____ing
_____gin
_____long
_____hind
_____side
_____tween
_____cause
_____fore
_____come

Exploring Hong Kong

millions

thousands

writing

China Chinese

signs

ong
Hong Kong
ping po_____
sing so_____
King Ko_____
stro_____
al_____

Hong Kong is a little bit of land and some islands on the east coast of China. Find it on your map.

Hong K_____ is a very small land and mil_____ of people live there. So the buildings are tall, the apartments where they live are t_____ , the office blocks and shops _____ big.

Why? _____

People in Hong Kong speak Ch_____se or English. TV has Chinese and English channels. Newspapers and street signs are also in Chin_____ and Eng_____ .

Hong Kong has many small islands and lots of harbors for thousands of b_____ts . There are Chinese junks that have sails and carry cargo. There a_____ sampans which are covered, and people live on them. Some sampans are floating shops which sell rice, vegetables, tea and milk.

Which is the sampan and which is the junk? How do you know?

Entertaining

Greece	Greeks
Rome	Romans
Egypt	Egyptians
China	Chinese

entertain

_____ment

_____ing

_____ed

flute

lyre

lute

harp

The Egyptians

ancient

cymbals

in stru ments
instruments

u–e

lute

fl__t__

__s__

am__s__d

__s__ful

prod__c__

t__n__ful

For thousands of years, people have pl____ed different kinds of mus____al instruments. Still today, we like to be enter_____ by lis_____ to music. In ancient days, the mu_____ instr_____ were not very diffe_____ from the ones we use today. They produced tune____ sounds.

Some of these inst_____ prod_____ sounds by blowing. The "pan pipes" from ancient Gre_____ and the flutes from Eg_____ were blown. They were made from reeds or bamboo.

Some sounds were pr_____ by plucking strings. The harp was used by the Gr_____, the Eg_____ and the Ro_____. The lute also had str_____ to pluck and it had a sound box like our modern fiddles. The lyre was a bit like a small h_____.

Then there were the bangers and clashers. Chin_____, Gr_____ and R_____ liked cy_____ to clash. Drums were normally made by stretching animal skins over metal or wooden rings.

Follow the pattern.

music	musician		
magic	_____	politic	_____
electric	_____	mathematic	_____

Thinking

tion

nation

sec_____

fac_____

addi_____

fascina_____

_____

_____

s c issors

happened

fas c inating

c

slice

twi__e

ni__e

pri__e

pen__il

s__issors

__enter

pie__e

fas__inate

on__e

Do some thinking about this simple but fas_____ piece of paper. All you will need is a strip of p_____, some glue, a pencil, and sc_____.

First, give your strip a twist as in the ske_____ and gl___ it together. You ha_____ now made a Möbius Strip.

twist once

Second, take your pen_____ and start to make a line down the ce_____ of your strip. Don't lift your pencil – just keep go_____.

What happened? _____

Be thi_____ about why it happ_____.

Third, take your s_____ and cut along your pe_____ line. What's happened n_____?
_____ Fascinating stuff!

twist twice

ci   **ce**

pencil   peace

_____   _____

_____   _____

_____   _____

_____   _____

Now take another strip of p_____. This time tw_____ it twice before gl_____ing it. Slice it down the cen_____ as before. Can you predict what is going to h_____ before you cut?

What actu_____ happened? _____

Try to explain why._____

_____